I Am One

I Am One

PRAYERS FOR SINGLES

CAROL GREENE

AUGSBURG Publishing House • Minneapolis

I AM ONE
Prayers for Singles

Photos: Mimi Forsyth, 10; Minneapolis Star and Tribune, 20; Florence Sharp, 26, 52, 89; Jim Whitmer, 33; Doug Stewart, 40, 82, 99; Elizabeth Wood, 46; Dave Anderson, 59, 94; Dan Lefebvre, 66; Wallowitch, 76.

Library of Congress Cataloging-in-Publication Data

Greene, Carol.
    I Am One.

    Bibliography: p.
    1. Single people—Prayer-books and devotions—
English. I. Title.
BV4596.S5G74   1985   242'.84   85-23015
ISBN 0-8066-2186-9

Manufactured in the U.S.A.   APH 10-3191

1   2   3   4   5   6   7   8   9   0   1   2   3   4   5   6   7   8   9

for Dayna

Contents

A Matter of Counting

I AM single, Lord.
I am one in a society
that counts by twos.
To some that makes me afflicted,
a person to be pitied.
To some it makes me sinful,
a person to be distrusted.
To many it makes me awkward,
an uneven number that upsets the balance.

You know the truth, Lord.
You know that I am
afflicted, sinful, awkward,
but no more and no less so
than your other children,
and you hold out to me
the same grace, forgiveness, and love.

O Lord, I praise you,
because you count by ones,
because you count each one equally precious,
each one utterly yours.

See Romans 3:21-26.

Love Nobody Wants

IT SOMETIMES seems, my God,
as if I am filled with love
that nobody wants,
as if I am a tree
abloom with flowers and fruit
that will never gladden or nourish anyone.
Do you know how that feels, my God?

O my God, you do!
In the garden at the beginning of time,
in the wilderness of Moses,
at the cross and forever after,
you have reached out to us with love
and we have turned away from you.

And yet you do not give up.
With divine stubbornness,
with boundless generosity,
in eternal hope,
you reach out again and again.

O God who loves,
O God who is love,
train me in love like yours.

See Romans 5:6-11.

Longing

O LORD, I long for the day
when there will be love enough,
when no one must hide
or run away
or weep alone.
I long for the day
when no one must be outsider
or scapegoat or deprived
so that others may be insiders,
superior, sated.
I long for the day
when birds will soar
and beasts will dance
and even the stones will sing
and all creation will forever move
in the perfect pattern of love.
O Lord, Thy kingdom come!

See Isaiah 11:1-9.

A Complaint to the Shepherd

IT IS true, my Lord,
that sometimes I become angry
at the portion of life you have allotted me.
The pastures are not as green as they could be.
The waters are not all that still.
And it seems to me, sometimes,
that I want for a great deal.
I do fear evil
and I get tired of looking at
the bountifully laden tables of my enemies.

It is well for me, Lord,
that you listen as a Shepherd,
that you recognize my raging
as the frightened bleats of your lost sheep.

Rescue me, Lord,
from the shadow that surrounds me.
Set my feet firmly back
on the path that you have chosen for me.
Be my rod and my staff
and bring me rejoicing
to the knowledge of your goodness and mercy
forever.

See Psalm 23.

Belonging

O LORD, I am nobody,
a misfit, unnecessary, superfluous.
At least that is what the world
seems to say
sometimes.
And sometimes
I believe the world.

Claim me, Lord.
Put your mark on me.
O Lord, let me find my identity in you.

Thunder above the voices of the world.
Whisper in the lonely watches of the night:
"You are mine—
Mine at your birth, now, and forever,
mine by creation, mine by redemption,
mine!"

See Psalm 139.

In Praise of the Ordinary

THANK YOU, Lord, for ordinary things:
for thoughtfulness that warms me
and smiles that make me welcome;
for bright moments of communion with strangers
and the outstretched hand of a friend;
for gentle memories that come with evening
and hope that returns with the morning.

Thank you for the slant of sun on green leaves,
for blue shadows on snow,
and the buoyant bird;
for the secret message of a shell
and the patient silence of the stars.

For these and a thousand other ordinary things
I praise you,
but above all
for making the ordinary
so special.

See Psalm 147.

Pettiness

MY SAVIOR,
who has taken upon yourself
the full measure of human anguish,
forgive me
when I allow the sting of petty hurts
to waste even one moment
of the new life you have given me.

Grant me perspective to see
where pettiness gets its sting—
in wounded pride, envy, self-pity.
And grant me a large enough vision
to brush the sting aside,
by turning my eyes away from myself
and toward you.

See 1 Peter 2:1-6.

Friendship

LORD JESUS, who has called me "friend,"
teach me the holy art of friendship.

As you love courageously—
   risking all to reach out to me—
   grant me a courageous love,
   willing to reach out to others.
As you love wisely—
   knowing all my needs—
   grant me a wise love,
   able to see the needs of others.
As you love cheerfully—
   gladdening my grayest moments—
   grant me a cheerful love,
   quick to gladden others.
As you love faithfully—
   forgiving all my trespasses—
   grant me a faithful love,
   ready to forgive others.
As you love selflessly—
   offering your life for me—
   grant me a selfless love,
   eager to live for others.

And as you are present in love—
   all the moments of my life—
   grant me a love that knows
   how to be present to others.

Lord Jesus, help me view friendship—
   your royal gift to me—
   as a special form of love;
let me embrace its high calling
as you embraced yours to be friend to me.

See John 15:11-17.

"The Least of These"

"WHATEVER you did for one of the least of these . . . .
you did for me"   Matthew 25:40.

It is comfortable, Lord,
to think of myself
as "one of the least of these."
Secure in my claim
of spiritual hunger,
spiritual nakedness, and homelessness,
I don't have to do anything.
I can wait for others
to feed and clothe and welcome me.

But that pricking spur of your Spirit, Lord,
won't leave me in comfort.
It pays no attention to my claims.
Instead
it shows me pictures
of starving people,
rag-wrapped children,
homeless families
and it demands:
"Do it! For me!"

See Matthew 25:31-46.

Vows

WHAT HAVE I to do with vows, Lord?
What can they mean to someone alone?
Just this:
that you have vowed to be my God—
in a rainbow-colored covenant
and in a covenant carried on a cross.

And so, Lord, let me make a covenant too.
Let me vow to be one of your people,
a minister of your royal priesthood,
garbed in rainbow and cross,
now, Lord, and forever.

O Lord, keep me faithful!

See Ephesians 2:17-22.

The Darkest Hour . . .

IN THE darkest hour, Christ,
when everything is wilderness
and I am alone,
when the pit opens before me
and there is no one to call me back,
when I understand that hearts can break
and don't know what to do for mine,
then, Christ, be with me.

Feed me with the holy bread
only found in wilderness.
Speak to me in the pit
and perhaps touch my hand.
And if my heart must break,
then, Christ,
let it break into your hands,
for you alone are God
and will make all things new.

See Romans 8:31-39.

Barriers

LORD, WHO am I?
I never used to think of myself
as anyone but myself,
me during childhood, adolescence, young adulthood,
me doing what everyone else did.

Now I am a "single," or an "un-married."
I am unwelcome at parties of former friends,
on vacations with "price based on double occupancy,"
and at my church's couples' club.
Instead I am encouraged to visit singles' bars,
take singles' cruises, and
join a singles' support group.

They seem so alien, Lord,
these new barriers,
because I am still me.
I still care what happens to my former friends.
I want to vacation with all kinds of people.
I want to be in fellowship with couples too.
But what is the worst, Lord,
is what the barriers do to me—inside.
They make me too cautious, too ready to retreat,
too quick to defend myself,
too eager to insist, "I am as good as anyone."
They alienate me from myself, Lord,
these alien barriers.

Smash them, Lord,
or, if that is not your will,
then make me wise as the serpent
to creep around them,
gentle as the dove
to fly above them.

See Matthew 10:16.

A Song Within

GIVE ME a song within, O God,
a psalm especially mine,
to sing in the face of joy or sorrow,
at home or in an alien land;
a song that beats steadfast as your faithfulness,
that soars high as your love;
a song to touch the heart of friend and stranger
and to speak to me when I am alone;
a song to sing solo throughout my life
and to join with angelsong beyond the grave.

See Psalm 149.

Your Plan

I ASSUME, Lord, that my singleness
is part of your plan for me,
at least for the moment.
But, that being the case,
I wish you had created me
with an extra pair of hands.

True, this solution might bring
problems of its own.
But do you realize, Lord,
how difficult it can be
with just two hands
to put one finger on the string and tie a knot,
to hold the cat and give it a pill,
to steady the ladder and clean the gutters?
Then there's turning the mattress,
putting a leaf in the table,
changing a—well, you get the idea.

I doubt that in your wisdom
you'll grant me additional appendages now.
But might I at least ask for
an extra portion of ingenuity?

See Psalm 33:1-11.

Wounds

I HAVE been wounded, Lord.
Big deal. Who hasn't?
The problem, I suspect,
is not so much my wounds
as this predisposition I have to lick them.
True, they are *my* wounds,
important to me,
and, I am told, important to you.
But can't I do something more constructive with them?

What about you, Lord, most grievously wounded?
You used those wounds,
scarlet badges of your compassion,
to fling wide the gates of heaven.

Use my wounds too.
Let the patience and understanding
I spend on my own pain
reach out in compassion
to the pain of others.
Then bless the touching, Lord,
with your healing hand.

See Isaiah 52:13—53:12.

The Prodigal

HERE I AM, Father, on the road again,
Your prodigal child, covered with dust.

Somehow I thought it would be different this time,
as I flew to the places where the lonely gather
and huddle together for warmth.
But of course it was no different.
We wore the fine feathers,
danced the mating rites,
sang the hollow songs,
and, Father, there was no warmth.

So here I am again, peering through the dust,
wondering if you're there, hoping for your welcome.
Now isn't that silly?
Of course you're there.
You're always there,
and here,
and in the places where the lonely gather,
ready to welcome,
waiting to warm.

See Luke 15:11-32.

To Believe

IF ONLY I could believe it, Lord—
that you are with me,
in all your love,
in all your power—
why, Lord, my life would be transformed!

No longer would I have to hide myself.
No longer would I have to defend myself.
No longer would I have to prove myself.
No longer would I have to sell myself.

If only I could believe it, Lord—
Lord, help my unbelief.

See Hebrews 11:1-16.

The Church

I SING of your church, Lord Christ,
the imperfect vessels, the broken clay,
your confused and stumbling, magnificent creation.
I sing of the old who comfort one another,
of the widows who wipe one another's tears.
I sing of the children, tumbling through dreams,
and the young not yet ready to compromise.
I sing of those who float your praise on golden melody,
and those who growl off-key,
and those who sing in silence.
I sing spaghetti suppers and soup kitchens,
coffee and juice and the feast at your table.
I sing the smug and the shy and the sorrowing,
the searching, the cynical, and the wise.
I sing of your sisters and brothers, Lord Christ,
your priests, your penitents, your redeemed.

See 1 Peter 2:9-10.

The Cost of Ministry

THESE DREAMS and visions of ministry
can be fearsome things, my Lord,
even when sent by your Spirit,
especially when sent by your Spirit.
You see, Lord, they demand so much
that I'm afraid they might consume me.
Sometimes I'd prefer a tamer challenge,
one that doesn't ask quite all of me.

But I believe you spoke to that issue, Lord—
something about losing and finding life.
So, Lord, preserve me from stinginess,
from being too careful with myself,
from hoarding my energies too closely,
and meting out my enthusiasm in measured doses.

Spur me to spend myself freely in your service,
to chase with the dreams and ride the visions.
Then, Lord, when I am spent,
renew me.

See Matthew 10:37-39.

Tired

IT IRRITATES me, Lord,
when my body fails me,
when I tire too soon,
ache too much,
look my age.
Perhaps there is something about being single
that makes me demand more than I should.
Or perhaps it's just part of being human
in a society that worships youth and beauty.
But I, Lord, profess to worship you
with my body
and all that I am.
So if I am clay,
and frail clay at that,
I am more too—
the vessel of your love and power
and these will never fail.

See 2 Corinthians 4:7-11.

Hymn to the Creator

O LORD, I have drenched myself in the splendor
   of your world!
I have breathed in sunrises and sighed out sunsets.
I have danced in the dew and the rain.
I have feasted on the comings and goings
   of your creatures:
the scurries of beasts,
slips of fish,
soars of birds.
Before me you have spread tapestries of flowers,
   oceans, skies.
I have tried to count the snowflakes and the stars
and laughed at my own folly.
Reflected in all you have made, O Lord,
is a truth that is also mine:
I, too, am one,
unique,
yours.
O Lord, I praise you!

See Psalm 104.

Fads

YOU SHOULD see us, Father,
when some new fad comes along,
how we rush to buy it,
wear it, read it, do it.
I suppose you do see us.
And what then?
Do you chuckle or sigh
at the sight of your creatures
scampering after some new salvation
when you have already given them all they need?
Fortunately fads are ephemeral things,
tripping over each other's heels
until even the dullest of us sees at last
that there is no salvation in them.
And when we turn, bewildered,
from the elusive and ephemeral,
remind us of all that is eternal.

See Philippians 4:8-9.

Competition

WHY DO we so foolishly persist
in regarding our life as a game?
Why must we struggle against one another
and count ourselves victorious
only when someone else has been defeated?
Why must we always have winners and losers
in the corporation,
the classroom,
the home,
and, yes, the church,
so that we are always divided,
always alone?
Father, I detest competition.
When I lose, I feel diminished in the eyes
    of others.
When I win, I am diminished in my own eyes.
How can I bring you offerings won
    from another's pain?
How can I serve Christ in someone I have trampled?
How can I hear the Spirit's voice over the noise
    of the game?
We face so many struggles in life.
Help us to struggle together.

See Galatians 6:2-5.

Withdrawal Symptoms

IT CAN be so easy, Lord,
for a person who is alone
to withdraw into a small, safe world
and slam the door behind.
There are no hurts in that world,
no rejections, no insecurities,
only the thick, sweet salve of routine
and the comfort of impenetrable walls.
It takes very little to live in that world,
only a tolerance of isolation
and an infinite capacity for boredom.

Deliver me, Lord,
from the temptations of that world.
Give me instead the courage required
to live a large life,
a generous life,
open to risk,
open to pain,
open.

See Galatians 5:1.

Death

for B.

JESUS, SAVIOR, it is done.
Gone now is the dearest one.
Hymns may shout of life begun;
I only know the dear one's gone.

Gone beyond my tenderest care,
Gone as far as whispered prayer.
Empty, empty hangs the air.
Gone now, Jesus, Savior—where?

To my vision, sad and slow,
Just a glimpse of heaven show.
Then, perhaps, I can let go
And wait, my Savior, wait—and know.

See John 14:1-6.

Grief

IT IS SEEING clearly that is so hard,
looking straight at death—
any kind of death—
and naming it: death.

It is holding still that is so hard,
standing quiet while waves of pain—
such raw, fierce pain—
ebb and flow, ebb and flow.

It is letting go that is so hard,
opening wide the hands, the heart—
still convulsed with love—
and surrendering what has been so dear.

And yet, Lord,
to look straight at death and name it
is to see beyond to resurrection;
to stand quiet in the waves of pain
is to hear your voice bid them be still;
and to let go is to surrender
no further than your waiting hands.

O Lord, give me courage!

See Psalm 46.

Birth

THE GRIEF has been hard, Father,
cold in the solitary chambers of night,
scorching in the senseless business of day.
I have looked out from a barren life
onto a barren land.
I have walked among people of stone
to whom death is an embarrassment.
I have longed for oblivion,
for any end to pain.

But almost imperceptibly, Father,
You sent the beginnings of peace.
Perhaps they first came when you gave me courage
to look at what was mortal
and so to see what is eternal.
And now, Father,
I feel the stirrings of hope,
such a tiny creature in so much darkness,
but one that whispers that the day is coming,
the day when you will change the anguish of never
into the triumph of forever.

See Psalm 121.

The Secret

SOMETIMES I can sense it, Father,
the great secret yet untold,
the hidden purpose that encompasses
all of life and death.

A scent,
a flickering,
a distant laughter.
Soon it is gone,
vanished into darkness
or invisible in light.

I plod on my lumpish way
through musings, reasons, words,
looking in all the wrong places
(if there are any wrong places)
for that which will not be found,
but only finds.

But there it is again!—
a hint,
an instant's certainty,
that Christ rules all of life and death,
and he is juggling the stars.

See Ephesians 1:2-10.

The Communion of Saints

SOMETIMES when I hear music,
or lose myself in a book,
or plunge my hands into rich, dark earth,
or close my eyes after your banquet—
sometimes I feel them all around me, Lord,
that vast Communion of Saints:
Elijah draped in awe and legend,
Isaiah fierce of eye,
sad Mary weeping in the garden,
Dorcas humming as she sews,
a nameless youth singing from the catacombs,
an archbishop kneeling in prayer,
a peasant girl arranging wheat and wildflowers,
a soldier crying in the night,
and all those living
and those yet unborn.
I hear their voices, hushed yet strong.
I see their outstretched hands, joined across centuries.
I feel their exultation and their pain.
Time is shattered
and I know I am a link in that great chain.

See John 17:20-23.

A Sanctuary

GRANT ME, Holy Father,
in the midst of all my busyness,
in the midst of the demands
the world makes of me
(and those I make of the world),
in the midst of the pain and the laughter,
the senseless chatter,
and the whole carousel of feelings
that toss me up and down—
grant me a little sanctuary,
a place set apart,
deep within,
inviolate.
In the stillness let me hear you.
Let me feel your power and your peace.
Let me find perspective,
set priorities.
Let me remember
who I am
and whose I am.

See Ezekiel 11:16-25.

Offerings

HERE THEY are, my God,
the offerings of this day:
delight in butter and orange juice
(please let there be orange juice in heaven),
a wastebasket full of crumpled papers,
three good sentences,
a watered garden,
tiny clawmarks, proof of a kitten's love
(please let there be animals in heaven),
righteous fury at a telephone solicitor,
a host of uncharitable thoughts,
a few kind ones,
three goals unmet and two accomplished,
a moment of song,
a moment of laughter
(there will be music and laughter in heaven?),
a gathering of friends,
and rest.
These are my day,
boring by some standards,
but I offer them to you, my God.
Use them as you will.

See Psalm 134.

48

Wings

WHEN I FLY to you, Lord God,
when the sky darkens
and the storm crackles round
and suddenly my wings seem very small,
then take me in, Lord God,
and hold me safe
beneath the great wings of your love.
Still my trembling,
ease my fear.
But do not let me stay too long,
for there is great need out there in the storm—
great need, Lord God,
and great beauty.
Strengthen my wings
that I may soar.
Strengthen me
that I may serve and celebrate.
Then, Lord God,
let me go.

See Psalm 91.

Self-analysis

I SPENT a lot of time, Lord,
looking carefully at this person
who is me.
I named any number
of my faults and phobias,
bad habits, neurotic tendencies,
and not-so-charming eccentricities.
Carefully I sorted out
just who was responsible for each,
where my parents went wrong,
where sibling rivalry entered in,
where I reacted inappropriately,
and all the rest.
(I hated that.)
Then I tried to understand the reasons
behind everything that happened
and from understanding moved
to forgiveness.
(That felt good.)

But now at last I am left with this person
who is me
and I think it is time
to accept myself,
faults, phobias, not-so-charming eccentricities,
and all.
Lord, you accept me just as I am.
Help me to do the same.

See Psalm 116.

The Escort

FOR ME, Lord Christ, one of the difficulties
     of being single
is that sometimes I must go places alone.
There are movies, concerts, ballgames, plays,
and friends are not always at hand.
Worse yet are funerals, weddings, and other events
where families seem to cling close together.
Sometimes I go anyway, Lord,
and sometimes it hurts.
Sometimes I stay home
and that hurts too.
It is fear that holds me back, I know,
and such a foolish fear to bring to you,
who traveled that Friday road without human
     companion,
and all for love of me.
But, shamefaced, I bring it anyway, Lord Christ,
and leave it and come away cheered
that he who walked to the cross with you
will accompany me wherever I go.

See John 16:31-33.

Failure

"THE WORST part," he said to me,
"must be the sense of failure,
of knowing that nobody wants you."
It was a cruel thing to say
made all the more so because
it was so easy to accept.
But his comment did not hurt as much
as once it would have.
At long last I have learned, Father,
not to recoil from failure,
but to accept it,
even as I accept success,
and to offer both to you.
I even suspect that from your point of view
some of my successes may be failures,
some of my failures successes.
But since I cannot reach your perspective,
I simply trust that you will use both—
my failures and successes—
to accomplish your will
and that is enough.

See Romans 8:28-30.

Cynicism

I DO not recall, Lord,
if it is one of the seven deadly sins,
but please preserve me from cynicism.
To be sure, it has its uses.
Pain, oppression, and all the aspects of sin
lose some of their power to hurt
if I can simply proclaim in a cool voice
that they are inevitable,
only to be expected,
considering the circumstances.
Besides, it is so sophisticated to be cynical.
But cynicism, I suspect, is more than a dodge.
It is also a canker
that eats at the root of faith
and blights the small bloom of hope.
So, Lord, even though it is comfortable,
please preserve me from cynicism.

See Ecclesiastes 1:12-15; 12:13-14.

Surprises

I PRAISE you, Lord, for surprises,
for all that should not happen,
but does:
the rose in November,
the child's impetuous kiss,
the unguarded look of love,
the dream that hints of heaven.
I praise you for all that I do not deserve,
but receive:
a moment's honor,
a friend's forgiveness,
an immortal instant outside myself,
a banquet of bread and wine.
I praise you for all that lies ahead,
promised, but still surprising:
days golden with your providence,
years kindled with your love,
a gathering of blessings,
and at last,
salvation for eternity.
O Lord, I praise you for your grace.

See Romans 5:1-5.

Rights

WE ARE all of us very concerned
about our rights today, Lord,
and while there is nothing wrong with that,
sometimes our defensiveness overwhelms us.
We speak only in strident voices
and forget to listen.
We cultivate aggressiveness
and forget to be gentle.
We clutch for power
and forget to serve.
In our quest for justice, Lord,
help us to remember your chosen Servant,
sent to proclaim your justice to all the world.
He rarely raised his voice,
was gentle with the weak,
yielded up his power,
and triumphed from a cross.

See Matthew 12:15-21.

A Wasted Day

IT'S BEEN one of those days, Lord.
I've moped from chore to chore,
no zip, no zest, no nothing.
And now as the sun floods the evening
with butter-yellow streams of light,
I ask myself how.
How could I have wasted this day?
Oh, not that I didn't accomplish things.
But not even once did I rejoice.
I draped this glorious day with my own clouds
and refused to let anything penetrate them.
And now I repent because this day is gone,
this unique, this beautiful day.
Dear Lord, who holds all our days in your hands,
don't let me ever waste another.

See Psalm 65.

Alive

TODAY
I watched a kitten chasing her own tail
in an absolute frenzy of play.
I watched a dog roll over and over in the grass
and wave his paws at the sun.
I saw a bird splash like a tiny typhoon
in the somewhat murky waters of my birdbath.
And I saw a child spin in delight
from tree to tree to tree.
Each was alone.
Each was utterly abandoned
to the joy of being alive in your creation.
Lord, let me learn from them.

See Genesis 1:26-31.

Self-realization

"I'M LOOKING for self-realization."
"I want to be my own person."
"I'm trying to fulfill myself."

We often say such things, Lord.
Sometimes it scares me.
I imagine this crazy picture of a bunch of buds,
running around on little root-legs,
trying desperately to turn themselves into flowers.

Often we talk about self-realization
when we want to run away from something,
like a responsibility
or a relationship.
We imagine some glorious place of total freedom
where we will blossom
into some new, better, happier person
and we run for it.
But I've never met anyone who's found it.

Is it true, Lord,
that buds cannot open
without the rich soil
of responsibilities and relationships?
Help us to realize your will,
to care more about one another
and less about ourselves.

See 1 John 3:13-24.

Judging

"As YOU judge others,
so you will yourselves be judged."
I used to think that was a threat
of divine retribution, Lord.
Now I'm not so sure.
It occurs to me that when I judge others,
I am usually defending myself.

X seems scornful of me.
Well, what do I care?
X is a stupid, conceited person.
That's how the thought process goes,
and at the end X is dismissed,
separated from me by my judgment.
X is no longer a threat.
She is separated from me.
But I am also separated from her.
So my judgment has been a two-edged sword.

"As you judge others,
so you will yourselves be judged."
Is it a threat, Lord,
or simply a description?

See Matthew 7:1-5.

Not Okay

"I'M OKAY. You're okay.
We're okay. They're okay."
Lies, Lord,
as you know well
and as any honest person must admit.

Take me, for example.
I'm not okay.
I do a great deal I shouldn't do
and don't do a great deal I should
and I doubt if there's a pure motive in me.

No, Lord, I'm not okay
and I don't know anyone who is.
But I am redeemed
and so are they.
That to me seems far better.

See Romans 7:14-25.

The Future

"TOMORROW WILL be better."
"I'll be happier next year."
"Maybe by Christmas . . ."

Honestly, Father, sometimes I remind myself
of a bird dog,
always pointing ahead,
always straining toward the future.
Not that a little hope for better things to come
isn't good for the soul.
But looking only forward
can be a lot like wearing blinders
and the fact of the matter is
that I am living *now*.

Strip off my blinders, Father.
Point me at the present.
There is so much I shouldn't be missing!

See Luke 4:14-21.

Angels

WE NEVER mention angels anymore, Lord.
To speak of them would probably embarrass us.
Perhaps they are too large for our reasonable views.
Their place is in the past, in tales of wonder,
not in the complexity of present-day events.
We do allow them space in children's books,
on Christmas cards and sometimes stained-glass
    windows,
but only as symbols,
pretty, but powerless, we think.
Still,
there are times,
hours, instants,
when
something very wrong inexplicably goes right,
an almost-sure disaster is suddenly averted,
a time of bitter loneliness is transformed into joy,
the basest of your creatures turns around and
    does great good.
I suspect we lack the courage to meet them
    face to face,
but, Lord, keep sending angels in whatever
    form you choose,
to proclaim again your glory to the heavens,
and to demonstrate your peace to all the earth.

See Hebrews 13:2.

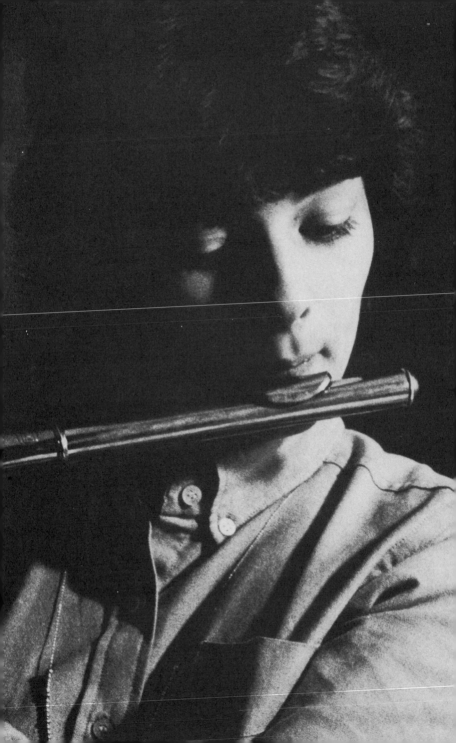

Missing Dreams

WHERE HAVE they gone, Lord,
those dreams of mine—
some large, some small,
some misplaced or broken,
some dimmed, forgotten,
some died a-borning—
where have they gone?
I cannot believe
that even the smallest of them,
sprouted from my most imperfect love,
is lost forever, O God of love.
Rather, I feel certain
that you hold them in trust for me,
a stored-up treasure
in that kingdom free of moth and rust,
till the day when I shall see them again,
bright and shining.

See Matthew 6:19-21.

Ambitions

O LORD, there is so much I want to give,
so much I want to do.
I want my time on earth to count for something.
I want to weave a golden thread
into the fabric of humankind,
to enrich the pattern,
to strengthen the cloth.
I really do!

Hold on to me, Lord,
when I float on such ambitious clouds,
and if I must fall,
let me fall gently.
Set me down in the places
where you would have me serve.
And if my offering is to be
no more than a widow's mite,
then let it be given nevertheless
with my whole heart
and to your glory.

See Hebrews 13:20-21.

Peace

WHEN I am restless, Lord,
discontented with what is,
regretting what might have been,
longing for what yet might be,
then give me peace.

Calm my anxious heart,
my groping hands,
my searching eyes,
and give me peace.

Let me hear as Mary did
the simple proclamation of your presence,
the banishment of fear,
the wonder of your plan.
Let me say with her, "So be it,"
and then I shall have peace.

See Luke 1:26-38.

Wilderness

I AM bewildered, Father.
When I look at this world
and the evil that stalks it,
I feel like one small speck,
lost and helpless in a wilderness.
I hear the cries of the victims
and see the smugness of their oppressors,
who are, perhaps, themselves victims
in another way.
And I ache with the pity of it all
and tremble with the horror,
until I must close my eyes and my ears
because I cannot bear any more.

O Father of Israel, our Father,
be with us once more in the wilderness.
Be with us—
and act with love and great power.
Let the wilderness bloom once again.

See Isaiah 55:12-13.

Holidays

WHEN I was a child, Lord,
I thought of holidays as wildly happy times,
bright golden bubbles
strung among the ordinary days.
Now, though, I am wary of them.
I recognize their fragility.
I know how easily bubbles can pop.
Loneliness is the real villain,
loneliness and sometimes my sense of failure,
especially when I see others in families
and I am alone.
Perhaps the bubbles are gone forever, Lord,
but I won't give up the holidays,
at least not the holy days
that point to your great acts.
Let your Spirit guide me, Lord,
beyond the wild but fragile happiness
to that quiet, tougher joy
with which countless generations
have celebrated your love.

See Psalm 122.

The Circle

IT HAPPENED at a party, Lord,
an outdoor party,
not so different perhaps from that long ago wedding
at Cana.

They formed a circle,
all the married ones,
and somehow forgot to include me.
Immediately this became for me
a powerful symbol
of so much that has happened in my life.
I felt rage, bitterness,
and—yes, Lord—hatred.

But then some small movement
(I don't even know what it was)
drew my eyes away from the circle,
and I looked around
at the stretch of grass,
the tall, straight trees,
the blue bowl of sky.

All at once I felt not excluded,
but free,
gloriously free.
And for that moment, Lord,
I praised you
in my assembly of one.

See John 3:8.

The Marketplace

DEAR GOD, I am weary of the marketplace,
of buying all those goods
that promise so much
and deliver so little.
I am sick of the scripture of advertising,
forever assuring me
that my deepest needs will be met at once,
if I only purchase the proper products.
But most of all, dear God,
I am tired to death
of stepping on the block myself,
of cultivating every superficial charm
and neglecting those parts of me
which yearn to grow,
of pretending to be something I am not
and denying who and what I am.
Perhaps I am out of touch
with the ways of the world.
Perhaps I should be enjoying
this so-called game.
But I am only weary
and I wonder, dear God,
if you did not create us for something better.

See Isaiah 55:1-5.

Lessons

LET ME learn of you, Lord Christ.

Let me learn to walk as you did,
sometimes singly,
sometimes with friends,
but always in company with the Father.

Let me learn to see as you did,
through the world's judgments,
through pain and sin,
to the child of the Father in each person.

Let me learn to care as you did,
without holding back,
without counting cost,
an open channel of the Father's love.

Let me learn to pray as you did,
in quiet simplicity,
in full trust,
to the Father who welcomes all his children.

Let me learn to die as you did,
to self and to selfishness,
to sin and to death,
wanting only to do the Father's will.

Let me learn of you, Lord Christ,
every lesson that you will teach,
because in the learning I will grow
closer to you and the Father.

See John 12:20-36.

Too Sensitive

DON'T let me be too tender, Lord,
too sensitive of skin,
too ready to take offense
(even when offense is meant),
too quick to slam down barriers
and hide behind them with hurt feelings.
A certain cheerful toughness
is what I'd like, my Lord,
off which the slings and arrows,
which still abound, may bounce.
A certain cheerful toughness
and the ability
(in Luther's words)
"to put the best construction on everything,"
not only to smooth my own path,
but to keep me open
to the paths of others.
And if in my cheerfulness
I miss an insult,
or if I put the best construction
on something deserving the worst—
well, who knows what might come of it?
That I can leave up to you.

See 2 Corinthians 6:3-10.

Good Times

I SUPPOSE it began in the garden, Lord,
when we chose to do it our way instead of yours,
and ever since we tend to leave you alone
until we are in desperate need.
Then back we scurry with our pain,
certain you will be there to strengthen and comfort,
and of course you are.
Perhaps it is my own aloneness that makes me see
how unfair this pattern of behavior is
to you and to us,
how much we withhold from you
and how much we miss
when we do not make you part of our good times too.
Help me break this pattern in my life.
Nudge me until I remember to invite you
to my parties as well as my wakes.

See John 2:1-2.

The Cross

"TAKE UP your cross," you said, Lord Christ,
and I ask you, "What is my cross?"
Is it being alone?
Is it loneliness?
Is it something I have done,
or something done to me?
Is it inside me or outside me or both?
Is it specific or general?
Does it remain constant or change?
I wish you had been a little clearer, Lord Christ.
I would prefer to name that cross
as I name the color of my hair and eyes.
But since you were not,
I will simply take up
all that I am and know and feel
and try to follow you.

See Mark 8:34.

Folly

THEY CALL me a fool, Lord,
and snigger at me behind their hands.
"Of course she clings to God," they say.
"What else has she got?
Another old maid, drunk on religion."

Lord, you put this collar on me,
and when I tried to run away,
You pulled me back.
You did not protect my pride,
but let it be battered by those who despise me.
You forced me to leave it behind in the dust
and follow, follow you.
And still you pursue me,
until I am ensnared by your love.

Lord, this road you have chosen for me
may not always be pretty,
but we walk it together, you and I.
And so for me it has the beauty of holiness.

See Jeremiah 20:7-13.

A Small Act

DEAR LORD, I fed the birds today.
Such a small act,
sliding a few steps from my door
to send seed bouncing across an icy lawn.
And now that they have eaten,
my little fir tree shakes with the symphony
    of their thanks,
until the gray skies dripping seem the lie
and I think it must be May.
This is wonder enough for one day.
Thank you. I am content.

See Mark 4:30-32.

Accepting Love

WHY IS it so difficult, Lord,
for me to accept love?
Why must I doubt it,
study it, test it?
Why can't I believe it's really mine?
Yes, Lord, I even question your love
sometimes.
Insignificant cipher that I am,
how could you love me?
But perhaps if I could ever get that part right,
could realize once and for all
what I mean to you,
then the other loves would fall into place.
No, Lord, I'm afraid it isn't enough
that you love me.
I need you to help me know it too.

See Ephesians 3:14-21.

Love

FOR ALL who have loved me,
for all who do love me,
for all who will love me,
for all I have loved
and do love and will love,
and especially for your love,
the true source of all love,
I thank you, O Lord, my God.

See 2 John 4–6.

Change of Perspective

WHEN I have had a bit too much
of my own company,
when I cry too easily and too long,
when the whine in my voice
drowns out the music,
then, Lord, let me laugh.
Lift me above my world
so I can sort out the silliness.
Get me beside myself
so I can see myself
and poke the necessary bit of fun.
From your perspective, Lord,
I must be quite a clown sometimes.
So let me share your vision
and laugh.

See Matthew 11:16-19.

Night

WHEN THE night is too cold or too hot,
when shadows gather at the foot of my bed
and fever burns behind my eyes,
when past pain and future fear dance like spectres
and my mind whirls out of control,
then come, Holy Spirit, to my aid.
Speak to me in whispers.
Touch my eyes and my heart.
Cool the fever,
banish the phantoms,
and guide me into wholesome sleep,
blessed with dreams of heaven
and the certainty of love.
Then, Spirit, when the night is gone,
wake me in joy
to serve again.

See John 14:16-17.

Betrayal

I COME to you, Lord, with a heart so bitter,
so filled with anger and pain,
that I do not even know if I can pray.
I have been betrayed, Lord.
Someone I love,
someone who loved me,
has rejected me,
cast me off.
Our relationship is broken
and nothing that I say or do
can ever make it whole again.
I am not wanted, Lord.
This person I love does not want me.
Such a simple truth.
Such searing pain.
No, Lord, I cannot even pray,
except to say,
please help me.

See Psalm 55.

The Heart

WHAT FRIGHTENS me most about pain, Father,
is that too much might dry up my heart,
turn it to stone, a barren place,
where nothing can live or grow.
And that, Father, seems to me
to be death
or even something worse.
Preserve me, Father, from death in life.
Let that of you which lives in my heart
be so deeply rooted, so strong and sound,
that nothing can ever destroy it.
Nourish it, Father, with the water of life,
especially in long, dry seasons,
and whatever harvests it may someday bear
I will offer in thanksgiving for your love.

See Ezekiel 17:22-24.

The Whisper

I LOOK back now, Father, on the worst moments,
when, like Joseph, I lay at the bottom of the pit,
hurt, helpless, alone,
unable even to ease the pain by putting it into words.
It was then, Father,
when I had no defenses of my own,
when I waited, utterly vulnerable,
for each new wave of pain,
that I felt the whisper,
too gentle to be heard,
yet sounding to the heavens,
the whisper that spoke what I could not say,
"Abba? Daddy?"
How I held on to that whisper, Father,
so tiny, yet implying by its very existence
that there might be someone to answer.
I see it now in symbols—
a silver cross, the shadow of a bird, a compass,
leading me limping but at last
into the kingdom of heaven.

See Romans 8:14-27.

Complexity

OURS IS such a complex world, Lord,
a world of intricate interrelationships,
complicated technologies,
and, yes, immense problems.
It is easy for a single human being
to get lost in such a world,
to feel insignificant,
impotent,
superfluous.
When these feelings threaten to overwhelm me,
take hold of me, Lord.
Turn me around
until I see again the basic things,
the important things,
the eternal things:
faith, hope, and love.
In the midst of this complex world, Lord,
grant me the gift of simplicity.

See 1 Corinthians 13.

The Financial Fidgets

I SIT here with my checkbook, Father,
juggling and balancing,
adding and subtracting
(mostly subtracting),
and worrying
as if my life depended on it.
"There is no one else,"
runs the refrain in my mind.
"I've got to take care of myself."

Why, *why* is it so hard to believe, Father,
that you will provide as you have promised?
Where is that exalted Sunday-morning feeling,
the moment of faith I knew just last week?

Drench me with faith, Father!
Let it permeate all the moments of my life,
including the most mundane ones,
including those spent with the checkbook.
Help me to live as the child of my Father,
who provides for his own—with abundance.

See Matthew 6:24-34.

One Voice

ONE VOICE, Lord—
that is all I am:
one voice
to speak your blessing,
sing your glory,
protest the evil that corrupts your world;
one voice
to tell your wonders,
beg forgiveness,
offer comfort to the fainting heart;
one voice,
sometimes weak,
sometimes confused,
sometimes unheard in the noise of the storm;
one voice,
but not alone,
instead in chorus with your creation,
a great symphony
of petition, penitence, praise.
Lord, hear us.

See Psalm 34.

The Path

ALTHOUGH MY own path
may sometimes seem gloomy,
my direction uncertain,
my vision blurred,
Lord, let me step out with confidence.
Teach me to hide my weariness, my fears,
and all those personal shadows
that might darken the paths of others.
Let courage, faith, and joy
be my companions as I travel,
so I may walk in light
and so shed light for others.

See Romans 15:1-6.

Groups

THE WORLD is so ready, Lord,
to divide us into groups:
singles' groups, couples' clubs,
youth groups, senior citizens.
Perhaps a certain amount of this
is all right,
but, Lord, let your children never forget
that far more unites us
than must ever divide us.
In our churches, at least, let us be one,
the young cheering the old,
the old comforting the young,
singles and couples bearing one another's burdens,
celebrating one another's joys,
and all trying to be faithful to you
together.

See Philippians 2:1-11.

Sex

I SOMETIMES wonder, Lord,
if sex was such a good idea.
True, it can be glorious.
True, it is useful in the propagation of species.
But, Lord, the trouble it causes
and what an idol we have made of it!
It is an especially thorny problem
(as Paul well knew)
for a single person,
a problem we solve with more or less guilt,
more or less rationalization and satisfaction.
Nevertheless, there it is—sex,
one of your many gifts to us.
Help me to own it,
instead of letting it own me.
Help me to use it,
instead of letting it use me.
Help me to keep it,
as you would have me keep all your gifts,
in the context of your love.

See 1 Corinthians 6:12-20.

Welcome

AT MY birth,
at my Baptism,
and at the break of each new day,
you make me welcome, Father,
in your world.

"I am glad you are here,"
proclaim your Word and your wonders.
"Be at home in this place.
I made it for you."

Welcome.
Yes, I am welcome,
well come,
and I thank you, Father.
I am glad I am here too.

See Isaiah 44:1-2.

Getting Old

GETTING OLD—
the thought of it frightens me, Father.
Loss of movement, freedom,
control over my own life—
how will I be able to bear it?
I imagine yielding myself
to the hands of others, strangers,
who may well regard my care
as no more than a profit-making enterprise,
and I am chilled.
I picture giving up the things I love,
animals, books, work,
and my heart falters.
And the vision of sitting alone,
superfluous, unmissed, waiting to die—
no, Father, I cannot even think of it.
Still,
why should then be so different from now?
Am I really now as independent as I think?
Don't I rely on you for each day's breath,
and won't you be as reliable then
as you are now?

O Father, God of all my days,
help me yield them all to you.
Grant me certainty that when all else—
even dignity—
has been stripped away,
you will remain,
my Lord and Protector,
through life, through death,
and beyond.

See Psalm 71.

Remembering

So MANY went before me, Lord God,
nameless ones whose stories will never be told,
but who made tremendous sacrifices
that I might live a better life.
Some sailed the seas to a freer land,
their dreams bundled in with their modest goods.
Some trekked the wilderness in search of a space
where dreams could grow and bear fruit.
Some died while they were defending others,
so that their dreams could live.
And still their dreams whisper after them:
"For the children. We did it for the children."
Perhaps they were not saints, Lord God,
but when I, their child, look back on what they did,
I feel humble and proud.
And as I offer to you the fruits of my labor,
I remember and bless you
for all those mothers and fathers of the dream.

See Deuteronomy 26:1-11.

If Only

IF ONLY I had said this.
If only I had done that.
If only I had been different then,
what might I be now?

It's a painful exercise, Lord,
this sifting through past mistakes,
painful and perhaps not too productive.
You and I both know
there were a lot of mistakes.
But I seem to spend far more time
looking back on them than you do.

"Forget them, child!" you tell me.
"Don't you know that I am God?
I will do a new thing
and not in some abstract way.
I will *do* it—for you!"

See Isaiah 43:18-21.

Magic

I NO longer believe in magic, Father.
Gone are Santa and the Easter Bunny,
banished forever to the kingdom of Nostalgia,
their places preempted
by credit card Christmases
and broken resolutions to try the Easter sunrise
    service.

Gone are the princes and princesses,
the heroic quests,
and palace-perfect happily-ever-afters.
Our quests are corporate now
and our castles condominiums
(so much more convenient).
We make our own futures
and we do it with no aid
from chargers,
potions, or wise old women.

I no longer believe in magic, Father.
(I've learned that it's bad theology anyway.)
But sometimes at night,
in the unguarded moments before sleep,
I creep down deeper into my cocoon,
ponder what you have already done,
and wonder if some magic morning
I shall awake with wings.

See Psalm 114.

The Possession

POSSESS ME, Lord, though I protest,
though I make feeble noises
about freedom, self-determination,
and my inalienable, individual rights.
The fact is, these things make cold companions
when I stand at the edge of the abyss
and there is no one to pull me back.
Then, Lord, need opens wide my eyes
and I see the truth—
that I cannot be free,
cannot be wholly myself,
until I am wholly yours.
So possess me, Lord,
with all your might,
with all your love,
and I will say Amen!

See Romans 6:20-23.

Questions

A SEASON is almost past, Lord Christ,
and I will be glad when it is gone.
Too many deaths, too much pain
have shattered the world around me
and stood in stark contrast to the jewel-like days.
Too often I have asked you why
and listened in vain for your answer.
I am your creature, born to ask why.
I do not think you would have me stand
in mute submission.
And so I ask again.
Why?
Why this suffering?
Why did the little baby die?
Why did you take the young girl?
Why has cancer struck two of my friends,
people who have served you faithfully?
I have heard the pat answers, Lord Christ,
and the sophisticated contemporary theology
and none of it speaks truth to me.
I am left with why.

A season is almost past
and I will be glad when it is gone.
Some atavistic corner of my soul must think
that death will die with the season
or perhaps that an answer lies just ahead.

See Psalm 36:5-9.

Spring

I ORDERED them just the other day, Lord—
snowdrops, crocuses, tulips, daffodils—
at least two hundred bulbs.
And soon in the late October chill
I will patiently plant them all,
smiling as I think of spring
and the secret hidden in each small brown lump.
They cannot know or even guess
the glory that is waiting for them.
And neither, Lord, can I,
deep-buried as I am in earth.
But you who hold all seasons in your heart
must sometimes smile when you think of spring
and the resurrections waiting for us.

See John 20:1-18.

The Story of My Life

WHAT DO I see, Lord God,
when I leaf through the pages of my life?
A grinning lump of infant,
a laughing child,
an earnest adolescent,
and myself as I am now.
All this I see, and more.
I see you there, Lord God,
Author of my life,
Redeemer of each page,
Father, Lover, Defender, Friend,
who will complete this story
even as you began it—
in infinite love.

See Hosea 11:1-4, 8-9.

Biblical References

Genesis 1:26-31
Deuteronomy 26:1-11
Psalm 23
Psalm 33:1-11
Psalm 34
Psalm 36:5-9
Psalm 46
Psalm 55
Psalm 65
Psalm 71
Psalm 91
Psalm 104
Psalm 114
Psalm 116
Psalm 121
Psalm 122
Psalm 134
Psalm 139
Psalm 147
Psalm 149
Ecclesiastes 1:12-15; 12:13-14
Isaiah 11:7-9
Isaiah 43:18-21
Isaiah 44:1-2
Isaiah 52:13—53:12
Isaiah 55:1-5
Isaiah 55:12-13
Jeremiah 20:7-13
Ezekiel 11:16-25

Ezekiel 17:22-24
Hosea 11:1-4, 8-9
Matthew 6:19-21
Matthew 6:24-34
Matthew 7:1-5
Matthew 10:16
Matthew 10:37-39
Matthew 11:16-19
Matthew 12:15-21
Matthew 25:31-46
Mark 4:30-32
Mark 8:34
Luke 1:26-38
Luke 4:14-21
Luke 15:11-32
John 2:1-2
John 3:8
John 12:20-36
John 14:1-6
John 14:16-17
John 15:11-17
John 16:31-33
John 17:20-23
John 20:1-18
Romans 3:21-26
Romans 5:1-5
Romans 5:6-11
Romans 6:20-23
Romans 7:14-25
Romans 8:14-27
Romans 8:28-30
Romans 8:31-39
Romans 15:1-6

1 Corinthians 6:12-20
1 Corinthians 13
2 Corinthians 4:7-11
2 Corinthians 6:3-10
Galatians 5:1
Galatians 6:2-5
Ephesians 1:2-10
Ephesians 2:17-22
Ephesians 3:14-21
Philippians 2:1-11
Philippians 4:8-9
Hebrews 11:1-16
Hebrews 13:2
Hebrews 13:20-21
1 Peter 2:1-6
1 Peter 2:9-10
1 John 3:13-24
2 John 4–6